Blessings
by the Sea

Paintings by
CHARLES WYSOCKI

HARVEST HOUSE PUBLISHERS

EUGENE, OREGON

Blessings by the Sea

Text Copyright © 2003 by Harvest House Publishers
Eugene, Oregon 97402
www.harvesthousepublishers.com

Library of Congress Cataloging-in-Publication Data

Blessings by the sea / paintings by Charles Wysocki.
    p. cm.
  ISBN 0-7369-1199-5 (alk. paper)
 1. Christian life—Miscellanea. 2. Oceans—Religious
aspects—Christianity—Miscellanea. I. Wysocki, Charles.
  BV4513.B58 2003
  759.13—dc21

                    2003001826

Design and production by Garborg Design Works, Minneapolis, Minnesota

Harvest House Publishers has made every effort to trace the ownership of all poems and quotes. In the event of a question arising from the use of a poem or quote, we regret any error made and will be pleased to make the necessary correction in the future editions of this book.

Unless otherwise indicated, Scripture quotations are taken from the Holy Bible: New International Version®. NIV®. Copyright © 1973, 1978, 1984 by the International Bible Society. Used by permission of Zondervan Publishing House; and the King James Version.

Printed in Hong Kong

03 04 05 06 07 08 09 / NG / 7 6 5 4 3 2 1

When upon life's billows you are tempest tossed,
When you are discouraged, thinking all is lost,
Count your many blessings, name them one by one,
And it will surprise you what the Lord hath done.
Count your blessings, name them one by one,
Count your blessings, see what God hath done!
Count your blessings, name them one by one,
And it will surprise you what the Lord hath done.

—JOHNSON OATMAN, JR.

All we behold
is full of blessings.

—WILLIAM WORDSWORTH

Ten-year-old Tara could sense the image of her mother growing smaller as the space between them along the train tracks became greater. Marshall, with all of his seven years of wisdom, seemed to be taking this trip to Aunt Julia's house in stride. He sat back on the coach seats and ran his hands admiringly along the shiny, leather cushions.

Although it had been a year since her father's death, Tara was worried about leaving her mother. Wouldn't she be so lonely?

When their mother first suggested a three-month New England coast vacation to spend time with their father's aunt, Tara was not pleased.

"Aunt Julia raised your father. He adored her. And when you visited her as a little girl, you did too. This visit will be a gift. Just wait and see." Her mother had tried to cheer her up.

"I don't remember her at all. And the town is so small; I won't have room to breathe." Tara folded and forced her clothes into her suitcase, each action exaggerated. Her mother kissed her on the forehead.

❀❀❀

"Tara!" Marshall looked imploringly at his sister. He was mid-explanation of their destination and had once again forgotten the name of the town.

"Mercy. It's Mercy," she said reluctantly. "But that's a joke."

The porter took his cue and sat down next to the teary girl who twirled her golden hair nervously. "Now why is that a joke, my young friend?"

"It is the town of our banishment, that's why. Mother is sending us to go visit a stranger."

"Our dad thought of Aunt Julia as his mother. We'll even be staying in the house he grew up in!" Marshall explained with exuberance.

"Well then, I think this town sounds great." The porter

The Blessing of Family

*The righteous man leads a blameless life;
blessed are his children after him.*

THE BOOK OF PROVERBS

winked at Tara.

"Why is that?" Tara looked up for a moment, wanting a reason to feel better.

"Because wherever you have family, you have blessings. Just wait and see."

Just wait and see. Did all adults tuck this saying away to use when vagueness suited them? Tara looked out the window at the passing scenery and secretly prayed this vacation would be worth waiting for.

The happiest moments of my life have been the few

God has given us no greater blessing than that of belonging to a loving and loyal family—and it will be so, always and forever.

—Richard L. Evans

Our Heavenly Father, we thank You for this food, the roof above us, and for this family. Help us remember that a family is for growing up in, for going away from, and for coming back to. It is for loving concern, for helping each other through happy times and sad. With Your blessing, this family will always be together in our hearts and in our memories, giving each of us the strength to live our own lives and to be our own persons. Amen.

—Virginia Backus

which I have passed at home in the bosom of my family.

—Thomas Jefferson

Sometimes when you think you are done, it is just the edge of beginning…It is beyond the point when you think you are done that often something strong comes out.
—NATALIE GOLDBERG

The Blessing of Beginnings

A new beginning! We must learn to live each day, each hour, yes, each minute as a new beginning, as a unique opportunity to make everything new…Imagine that we could live each day as a day full of promises.
—HENRI J.M. NOUWEN

The waves echo behind me. Patience—Faith—Openness, is what the sea has to teach. Simplicity—Solitude—Intermittency…But there are other beaches to explore. There are more shells to find. This is only the beginning.
—ANNE MORROW LINDBERGH

He who chooses the beginning of a road chooses the place it leads to. It is the means that determine the end.
—HARRY EMERSON FOSDICK

"Wake up, Tara," Marshall prodded his sister while he struggled to pull his bag from the overhead shelf.

The carved red sign with white letters confirmed that the small train station was their introduction to the town of Mercy. Marshall looked out the window anxiously. Would he recognize Aunt Julia from the old, worn photo?

Tara was dazed as she wiped leftover tears from her sleepy eyes. For once she let Marshall lead the way. As the young travelers stepped onto the platform, a woman in overalls and a tan leather cap approached them.

"Aunt Julia?" Marshall asked quietly. He got his answer as she opened her arms wide to hug them and howled with delight. Within her embrace, the children smiled and recognized the sound of their father's laugh.

❁ ❁ ❁

Once in the horse carriage, Tara timidly perched in the back on a stack of blankets while Marshall sat right next to Aunt Julia. Feeling brave, he even asked a question. "Where is your striped stocking cap?"

"Did your father tell you about that thing? Well, I have a secret about that crazy cap." She leaned in but spoke loudly enough for Tara to hear. "Your father knitted it to show his sister that he could. He was so afraid his friends would find out. But I never told a soul. Until now, that is."

"You like hats, huh?" Marshall noted the one presently hovering over her head.

"What else is a gal to do with all of this?" Julia lifted the cap to reveal a mass of gold-yellow hair. Marshall looked at his sister and mouthed, "Do you see that?"

The Blessing of Belonging

I have summoned you by name; you are mine.
When you pass through the waters,
I will be with you.

THE BOOK OF ISAIAH

"It's my hair!" Tara was stunned. All these years she had been the only person in her family—in her county—with such hair.

"You had to get it from somewhere, sweetie!" Aunt Julia called over her shoulder. "One thing is for sure, everyone in town will know we belong to each other."

Tara held those words in her heart as she settled into the blankets. The thought of *belonging* was very comforting.

11

There shall be showers of blessing:
This is the promise of love.
—DANIEL W. WHITTLE

Nothing we do, however virtuous,
can be accomplished alone;
therefore we must be saved by love.
—REINHOLD NIEBUHR

I f we have no peace, it is because

A mere walk along the shore has exorcised the dreary state in which we found ourselves...a day that began in the doldrums has lightened up; one that began with us apart has ended with us together.
—JOAN ANDERSON
An Unfinished Marriage

we have forgotten that we belong to each other.

—MOTHER TERESA

Nature often holds up a mirror so we can see more clearly the ongoing processes of growth, renewal, and transformation in our lives.

—MARY ANN BRUSSAT

The Blessing of Renewal

Dawn has broken on a beautiful day here at the ocean. I've come to refresh my weary spirit and to refuel my tired soul. I'm so grateful for the peace and the calm of the seashore, where time stands still and unrushed...where I can see and feel the beauty all around me.

—CAROL HAMBLET ADAMS

Might I discover a stilling of the soul that invites God and a new recreation of life? Would I see that waiting, with all its quiet passion and hidden fire, is the real crucible of spiritual transformation?

—SUE MONK KIDD

Create in me a pure heart, O God, and renew a steadfast spirit within me.

THE BOOK OF PSALMS

Aunt Julia slowed the carriage to a halt by the local feed store. Marshall and Tara hopped out of the carriage and followed their great-aunt along the winding walkway toward a local inn. People greeted them by name along the way, and many stepped in behind them.

"How do they know us?" Marshall was impressed with his immediate popularity.

"I have been bragging about you two for so long, they were beginning to think I was losing my marbles. Your arrival today saved my reputation." Aunt Julia opened the large door for Marshall, but as Tara was about to enter, a large man with a

The Blessing of Community

But if we walk in the light, as he is in the light,
we have fellowship with one another.

THE BOOK OF 1 JOHN

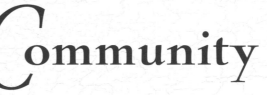

gray beard stepped between the ladies. Unlike the other townsfolk, his deep-set black eyes conveyed no friendly greeting.

"Julia." He spoke the word like a harsh sneeze.

"Hello, Mr. Winters. You look very fine today, sir." Aunt

Julia pointed behind him. "I'd like you to meet Tara—Michael's girl. His son, Marshall, is in the store. You'll likely see them walking along Valley Road during the next few months."

"Not near the orchards I hope." He barely glanced around at Tara. "Good day," he said a bit more softly but then turned and left quickly.

"He's scary," Tara whispered.

"You should have seen him back when he was mean!" Aunt Julia said good-naturedly, watching the man walk away, a look of empathy on her face.

"Helloooo," Marshall called through the screen door. "In case you didn't realize it…these people have a party going on in here! For *us!*" He disappeared inside as they followed. Grand centerpieces of large pumpkins and colorful leaves decorated each of the tables. Platters of pies and breads lined the long buffet. A chorus of "Welcome to Mercy" concluded the joyous collective prayer.

Tara tugged on the leg of Aunt Julia's overalls. "Why are they giving *us* a party?" With a twinge of guilt, Tara recalled her resistance to visit this place.

Aunt Julia kneeled down to be eye level with the girl. "They want to share with you the blessing of community. You show your appreciation by accepting it. So, what do you say?"

Though her first impulse was to mimic the phrase "I'll wait and see," she was beginning to realize how hungry she was for a blessing in her life.

I begin each day with a solitary early morning walk on the beach, during which I am often the only person in sight. I step on tide-washed sand and run my eye along the blue-gray eastern horizon between sea and sky. If I slice this line into segments, each appears to be straight, but the sweep of the whole curves to render the world perceptibly round. Just so, an individual life can appear to be isolated and without purpose unless recognized as contributing continuity to lives that precede it and follow it, endowing each human span with rich universality.

—Anne Truitt

For health and food,
For love and friends,
For everything Thy goodness sends,
Father in Heaven,
we thank Thee.

—Ralph Waldo Emerson

I am of the opinion that my life belongs to the whole community and as long as I can live it is my privilege to do for it whatever I can…I rejoice in life for its own sake. Life is no "brief candle" to me. It is a sort of splendid torch which I have got hold of for the moment, and I want to make it burn as brightly as possible before handing it on to future generations.

—George Bernard Shaw

Talking to yourself in those long breaths that
Sing or hum or whistle fullness of the heart,
Or the short breaths,
Beats of the heart,
Whether it be of sadness or a haystack,
Mirth or the smell of the sea,
A cloud or luck or love,
Any of these or none—
Is poetry.
—Witter Bynner

O Maker of the sea and sky,
Whose word the stormy winds fulfill,
On the wide ocean Thou art nigh,
Bidding these hearts of ours be still.
—Henry Burton

*Sit in reverie and watch the changing color of the
waves that break upon the idle seashore of the mind.*
—Henry Wadsworth Longfellow

There is a pleasure in the pathless woods,
There is a rapture on the lonely shore,
There is society, where none intrudes,
By the deep sea, and music in its roar:
I love not man the less, but Nature more.
—George Gordon, Lord Byron
Childe Harold's Pilgrimage, 1818

The Blessing of Solitude

*Small miracles are all around us. We can find them everywhere—in our
homes, in our daily activities, and, hardest to see, in ourselves.*
—Sue Bender

© Charles Wysocki

Aunt Julia lifted her arms out to the side and twirled around in her living room. "This humble home of mine is now your home as well. It isn't grand, but it is quite a wonderful place to live and dream." Marshall tried the twirl of hospitality while Tara watched with a bit of disbelief and stubbornness—she would not be thinking of this tiny beach shack as a home. And were grown women supposed to twirl like schoolgirls?

"Your rooms are at the top of the stairs. Watch out for the sloped ceiling." Her fingers barely pointed upward and Marshall was racing up the staircase.

"We get our own rooms?" Tara asked hopefully.

"Every young lady needs a room of her own."

"Will I be able to see the water from my window?" Tara asked.

"I'm afraid Marshall has the ocean view." She paused and tried to catch Tara's wandering gaze. "I gave you your father's old room instead." The young girl's face lit up. Her eyes watered; homesickness and heartsickness mingled with fatigue.

❀ ❀ ❀

"Tara, your room is great. But you should see my view!" Marshall jumped up and down on the small cot beneath a high portal window while his sister lingered at the small wooden desk covered with little stacks of papers. "Do you want to go and try to fly this kite? I'll bet it was dad's…"

Marshall touched the tail of a bright yellow and blue kite that hung from the slanted wooden beams.

Soon their father's old toy was riding waves of wind as the children ran in jagged patterns along the tide line and strained

The Blessing of Home

Blessed are those who dwell in your house;
they are ever praising you.

THE BOOK OF PSALMS

to catch their breath. "Dear brother," called Tara in a voice hoarse from laughing for several hours. "I do believe it is time to go home." Tara repeated the unexpected word, "Home?" But this word was reserved for the house back in Greenville where mother waited. Where father had kissed them goodnight. Where her Sunday dresses hung in an armoire her father had made…

"I know just what you mean. I feel it too. Can a person have two homes?" Marshall spoke with surprising perceptivity.

"It seems so, Marshall." Tara took one edge of the kite and helped her brother traverse the dune toward the cottage—the beach shack that had quickly taken on the look of home.

Stepping Ashore

Oh! Think to step ashore,
And find it heaven;
To clasp a hand outstretched,
And find it God's hand!
To breathe new air,
And that, celestial air;
To feel refreshed,
And find it immortality;
Ah, think to step from storm and stress
To one unbroken calm:
To awake and find it Home.
—Robert E. Selle

A red shimmer fell on the grass at Heidi's feet and she turned round. She had not remembered, even in her dreams, how beautiful this picture was...Far below stretched the valley, and above and around everything glittered and sparkled. Tears crept down Heidi's cheeks at the sight of all this splendor. Earnestly she pressed her hands together and thanked God for bringing her home again.
—Johanna Spyri
Heidi

Where we love is home—home that our feet may leave, but not our hearts.
—Oliver Wendell Holmes Sr.

A home is truly a blessing, a treasure more precious than we realize. Whatever home we have been blessed to own or rent or otherwise inhabit is quite simply a gift, and the simple hearted among us realize that good gifts are meant to be shared. Our homes should stand ready to welcome friends, kin, strangers, and pilgrims.
—Claire Cloninger

The meek, the merciful, even those who are persecuted—blessed, blessed, blessed.
Not later. Not when their trials are over. Not when they are fixed. Right here, right now.
There is a blessing for you here, now, in this very moment.

—WAYNE MULLER

The Blessing of Now

I live with the past,
not in it. I know I am
deeply nostalgic, but
my roots, which are
entwined in the world
of yesterday, are also a
natural bridge to the
world of today.

—CHARLES WYSOCKI

When the fiddle had stopped singing Laura called out softly, "What are days of auld lang syne, Pa?"

"They are the days of a long time ago, Laura," Pa said. "Go to sleep, now."

But Laura lay awake a little while, listening to Pa's fiddle softly playing and to the lonely sound of the wind in the Big Woods. She looked at Pa sitting on the bench by the hearth, the fire-light gleaming on his brown hair and beard and glistening on the honey-brown fiddle. She looked at Ma, gently rocking and knitting.

She thought to herself, "This is now."

She was glad that the cozy house, and Pa and Ma and the fire-light and the music, were now. They could not be forgotten, she thought, because now is now. It can never be a long time ago.

—LAURA INGALLS WILDER
Little House in the Big Woods

Overly concerned with what has been, stressed and consumed by what is yet to be, we tend to forget that life is happening in the immediacy of this instant...In surrender to the Spirit, now can become more than a holding pattern, a painful pause, or a frightening flight. It can become important. Significant. Fulfilling. Extraordinary. Sacred.

—KIM THOMAS
Living in the Sacred Now

The day was filled with many errands for Tara and Aunt Julia, from checking in on sick neighbors to buying chocolates for the evening's dessert.

"I have just one more thing on my list. I agreed to pick up flowers and deliver them to the chapel for the special end-of-summer service this week." As they pulled up to the flower cart, Tara turned her attention once again to the matter that had bothered her all day long. Aunt Julia's little finger had a piece of string tied around it. Surely it was there to trigger the older woman's memory…but after each errand, the knot remained.

Tara's curiosity turned into anxiety. Was her aunt forgetting one last task for the day? An important duty that remained unfinished? Still shy around her relative, Tara didn't want to ask and embarrass her aunt or herself, so every now and then she deliberately looked at the string as a subtle hint.

That didn't work.

Suppertime had arrived, and Tara added a last bit of lemon to the salmon they had baked. Aunt Julia went about her day, oblivious to the fact that something important had been neglected. She had not a care in the world as she spoke dramatically at the table about their day…the ends of the string flitting and floating with every gesture.

When bedtime snuck up on them, Aunt Julia yawned and covered her mouth with her string-adorned hand. Tara's shyness finally gave way to her concern. "For goodness sake, Aunt Julia…what important thing have you yet to do with your day?"

Aunt Julia stopped mid-yawn. "Whatever do you mean, Tara?" she asked, though her grandniece was already pointing specifically to the string. "Why, I have not forgotten a thing, my love." She lifted her hand and merrily wiggled her fingers. "This, my dear, is indeed to trigger my memory. It is to remind me to make the most of my time with you both so I can cherish it later."

"You mean…" started Marshall who was just beginning to understand the conversation, "the string is a reminder to

The Blessing of Memories

This is the day the LORD has made;
Let us rejoice and be glad in it.
THE BOOK OF PSALMS

remember a memory while you are making it?"

"I could not have explained it any better."

Tara giggled with great relief at her crazy aunt's idea—and a bit at herself for worrying. She pulled a strand of ribbon from her hair and tied it around her own finger.

"And what is it that you want to remember?" asked Aunt Julia with a smile.

"I want to remember the day you reminded me how to laugh again!"

Some memories are realities, and are better than anything that can ever happen to one again.
—WILLA CATHER

Be thankful for your blessings all:

The happy memories you recall;

For time, which every heartache mends,

And, oh, be thankful for your friends.

—EDGAR GUEST

To live in the past and future is easy. To live in the present is like threading a needle.
—WALKER PERCY

Every man's memory is his private literature.
—ALDOUS HUXLEY

My soul is full of longing for the secrets of the sea,
And the heart of the great ocean sends a thrilling pulse through me.
—HENRY WADSWORTH LONGFELLOW

The Blessing of Mystery

The most beautiful thing we can experience is the mysterious. It is the source of all true art and all science. He to whom this emotion is a stranger, who can no longer pause to wonder and stand rapt in awe, is as good as dead: his eyes are closed.
—ALBERT EINSTEIN

There is, one knows not what sweet mystery about this sea, whose gently awful stirrings seem to speak of some hidden soul beneath.

—HERMAN MELVILLE

33

After several weeks in Mercy, Tara knew every curve of sandy Valley Road, which led to town. Only occasionally did one encounter another resident along its stretches, so Tara was startled when she and Aunt Julia rounded the corner and bumped into Mr. Winters' carriage on the narrow road.

The Blessing of Giving and Receiving

It is more blessed to give than to receive.

THE BOOK OF ACTS

"What in the world!" Mr. Winters scowled his well-practiced scowl but changed his demeanor when he saw who it was. He adjusted his carriage and went on his way with a flick of the reigns and a slight nod of the head.

"Interesting that we should run into him here," said Aunt Julia, mostly to herself.

"Why is that?"

"I named this slice of my land Forgiveness Acres because of Mr. Winters."

"Did he hit your carriage here, too?"

Aunt Julia laughed but then became solemn, "You see, Mr. Winters owned this land before my husband purchased it. We paid what we could initially and then spent the next three years

working extra jobs to pay it off. When we made the final payment, Mr. Winters insisted that we still had another year to go."

"He is a mean man." Tara despised injustice. "You didn't pay him, did you?"

"We did because we had nothing to prove otherwise. This time, however, we put the agreement in writing. But sadly, just a few months later my husband died. I knew I would have to sell the land back to Mr. Winters."

"That's not fair!" Tara's face grew red.

"Well, I needed to honor the written contract, so I prepared to give up the land we loved so much." Aunt Julia paused briefly. "But before I could go see Mr. Winters, he showed up at my house with an awkward look, the deed to the acreage, and a year's worth of our payments. It was a very important moment."

"Well…it should have been yours anyway, right?"

"Yes. But I understood he was asking for forgiveness."

"Still…" Tara struggled to understand her aunt's gracious attitude.

"Tara…forgiveness is an exchanged gift. One must give and one must receive for it to be made complete. I forgave in memory of the godly man my husband was and in honor of the person Mr. Winters was trying to be."

After a long moment of silence, Tara assessed the situation, "I hope he knows what a huge gift forgiveness is."

"He knows, my dear. The sea is an ever-present reminder of the cycle of giving and receiving. When you live here it becomes second nature. Mr. Winters just needed to get back in the flow of things, that's all."

I will bless them and the places surrounding my hill. I will send down showers in season; there will be showers of blessing.

THE BOOK OF EZEKIEL

It is in pardoning that we are pardoned.

—SAINT FRANCIS OF ASSISI

Not what we say about our blessings, but how we use them, is the true measure of our thanksgiving.

—W.T. PURKISER

For every beauty there is an eye somewhere to see it.
For every truth there is an ear somewhere to hear it.
For every love there is a heart somewhere to receive it.

—IVAN PANIN

He that cannot forgive others, breaks the bridge over which he himself must pass if he would ever reach heaven, for everyone has need to be forgiven.

—GEORGE HERBERT

Forgiveness is the giving, and so the receiving, of life.

—GEORGE MACDONALD

The Blessing of Wisdom

Blessed is the man who finds wisdom,
> the man who gains understanding,

for she is more profitable than silver
> and yields better returns than gold.

She is more precious than rubies;
> nothing you desire can compare with her.

Long life is in her right hand;
> in her left hand are riches and honor.

Her ways are pleasant ways,
> and all her paths are peace.

She is a tree of life to those who embrace her;
> those who lay hold of her will be blessed.

The Book of Proverbs

The Blessing of Happiness

The morning light awakened Tara as it seeped into her father's childhood bedroom. The kite was back in place and cast birdlike shadows across the floor. Her father's drawings of the sea, of local wildlife, and of regal ships still covered the wood plank walls. She looked them over each morning, searching for something she would recognize as her father.

Today Tara focused on a drawing of the beach. As she looked intently at the sketched figures on the sand, she could make out a family of four. A boy, a girl, and parents walking ahead, holding hands. *How strange,* she thought, *it looks like our family.* Then she noticed the title her young father had given the piece—Happiness. She smiled. Her father had been blessed to see his vision of happiness realized during his lifetime.

Her bare feet led her over to the desk where she sat on the creaky chair and for the first time looked at the stacks of note papers. The handwriting was familiar… and as Tara unfolded the letters she understood why. They were notes from her mother to her father. The words reflected the growing friendship and love between the two young teenagers. Long ago Tara's mother had told her the story of how she met Tara's father while visiting Mercy.

The letters were confessions of falling in love with the small coastal town. "The constant, powerful presence of the water is a source of peace that I miss here in the city. I find that I long for the sea as the sun rises each morning. I look forward to getting to know the ocean as you do…as a friend, as a confidant, as a reminder of God's presence in our lives. Mercy was indeed a blessing to me, as is our friendship. 'Til I find a moment to write again, Sarah."

While Marshall slept soundly, Tara entered his room and looked out at the same sea that had brought their mother and father together. And with each rise of the waves, Tara felt her heart swell in proportion. For the first time in such a long time she felt happy and truly, truly blessed.

Let the heavens rejoice, let the earth be glad;
let the sea resound, and all that is in it.
THE BOOK OF PSALMS

In the intervals of the game, while Uncle Henry was pondering over his moves, the little girl looked down at her pets and listened absently to the keen autumnal wind that swept around the old house, shaking the shutters and rattling the windows. A stick of wood in the stove burned in two and fell together with a soft, whispering sound. The lamp cast a steady radiance on Uncle Henry bent seriously over the checkerboard, on Molly's blooming, round cheeks and bright hair, on Aunt Abigail's rosy, cheerful, wrinkled old face, and on Cousin Ann's quiet, clear, dark eyes….

That room was full to the brim of something beautiful, and Betsy knew what it was. Its name was Happiness.

—Dorothy Canfield Fisher
Understood Betsy

White in the sunshine her sails will be gleaming,
See, where my ship comes in;
At mast-head and peak her colors streaming,
Proudly she's sailing in;
Love, hope, and joy on her decks are cheering,
Music will welcome her glad appearing,
And her heart will sing at her stately nearing,
When my ship comes in.

—Robert J. Burdett

But may the righteous be glad
and rejoice before God;
may they be happy and joyful.

The Book of Psalms

His master replied, "Well done, good and faithful servant! You have been faithful with a few things; I will put you in charge of many things. Come and share your master's happiness!"

The Book of Matthew

The best and most beautiful things in the world cannot be seen or even touched. They must be felt with the heart.
HELEN KELLER

A thing of beauty is a joy forever; its loveliness increases; it will never pass into nothingness.

—JOHN KEATS

The Blessing of Beauty

Everybody needs beauty as well as bread, places to play in and pray in, where nature may heal and give strength to body and soul.
—JOHN MUIR

"Is there anything more beautiful than sunrise on the ocean?" Nan crept out of bed at the first peep of dawn, and, still in her white robe, she sat in the low window seat to see the sun rise, "under her window."

"What a beautiful place!" Nan thought when dawn gave her a chance to see Ocean Cliff. "Dorothy must be awfully happy here. To see the ocean from a bedroom window!" And she watched the streaks of dawn make maps on the waves. "If I were a writer, I would always put the ocean in my book," she told herself, "for there are so many children who never have a chance to see the wonderful world of water!"

—LAURA LEE HOPE
The Bobbsey Twins at the Seashore

Blessed are the
merciful,
for they will be
shown mercy.

THE BOOK OF MATTHEW

46

The Blessing of Mercy

The mercy of God is an ocean divine,
A boundless and fathomless flood.
Launch out in the deep, cut away the shore line,
And be lost in the fullness of God.
—ALBERT B. SIMPSON

The quality of mercy is not strained;

It droppeth as the gentle rain from heaven

Upon the place beneath. It is twice blessed—

It blesseth him that gives, and him that takes.

—WILLIAM SHAKESPEARE

The Blessing of Sharing a Blessing

We're "counting" the blessings, our joys we record,
The wonderful mercies like sunbeams outpoured;
But let us remember while praising the Lord,
Somebody else needs a blessing.

Somebody else needs a blessing,
Somebody else needs a blessing;
We'll let our lights shine to His glory divine,
Somebody else needs a blessing.

—ELIZA E. HEWITT